From Trauma
To Triumph

The black woman's journey to waking up happy every day!

By LeAnne Dolce

By LeAnne Dolce

Copyright © 2023 LeAnne Dolce

All rights reserved. No part of this book may be reproduced in any form without permission from the author or publisher, except as permitted by U.S. copyright law.

To request permission, contact:
LeAnne Dolce – hello@dolceandlay.com

ISBN: 978-0-9823328-1-8
Printed in United States
1st Edition

Published by Dolce & Lay, LLC
600 Bronner Brothers Way SW, Suite Y532,
Atlanta, GA 30310

TABLE OF CONTENTS

Introduction………………………..………………….4

Chapter 1
A Foundation in Self-Care……………….……..13

Chapter 2
It's Time to Get RADICAL about Black Women's Self-Care………….…….……….……….29

Chapter 3
Harnessing the Power of Your Feminine Energy……………………………………….46

Chapter 4
Healing From Past Trauma…………………..….63

Chapter 5
Healthy Boundaries as Healing Agents……..…..78

Chapter 6
The Gift of Unconditional Self-Love……….…..91

Chapter 7
I'm Not Your Superwoman……………....…….107

Chapter 8
Breaking Free from Narcissistic and Toxic
Relationships......................................…..119

Chapter 9
Your Ultimate Self-Care Toolkit.........…...…133

Conclusion..…..…150

Introduction

Many black women have experienced trauma in their lives, whether from racism, sexism, other forms of discrimination, hurt or even from well-meaning parents and authority figures. This trauma can often lead to feelings of worthlessness and powerlessness. However, it is possible to heal from this trauma and reclaim your sense of self-worth and power.

This book will guide you on how to do just that. We will explore topics such as the importance of self-care, forgiving yourself and others, setting healthy boundaries, and unconditional self-love. By working through these topics, you will begin to heal the wounds of your past and attract more love and joy into your life.

By LeAnne Dolce

If you are ready to start your journey to healing and wholeness, then this book is for you. Let us begin.

Healing from trauma is possible. Triumphant stories of healing and transformation abound, but often these stories are not shared by people of color. This book is a collection of essays written by a black woman who has journeyed through pain, heartache, and trauma to emerge victorious and whole. I hope that this book will offer readers courage, hope, and inspiration as they walk their Healing path.

This book is not just for black women, but for anyone who has faced trauma and abuse, who struggles with self-care or setting boundaries, who wants to heal from toxic relationships, and who longs to love themselves unconditionally.

I believe that when we love ourselves, love is attracted to us and that we all have the power to triumph over our traumas. No matter what we have been through, we can choose Healing, hope, joy, and love."

As Black Women, we are the foundations of our families. We are expected to always be happy or else we are seen as the "angry black woman". We don't feel like we are allowed to show weakness because we are the ones that everyone comes to for help, but no one checks on us to see if we need help. We want to honestly just wake up happy every day so that we can be healthy, healed, and whole. We want to heal from all the trauma that has been passed down and showered upon us. We want to show up confidently, unapologetically, and authentically happy. We want to ensure that we are teaching this to our children as we are the ones who will STOP the generational trauma that was passed to us. When we are happy, confident, and loving of ourselves, we bring more love and happiness to ourselves because love attracts love.

This is why I wrote this book; to share my learnings of trauma and Triumph. To give Black women a start on their journey of waking up happy every day. In these pages, you will find hope and healing for your life journey. You will learn how I reclaimed my life after years of pain and suffering. You will find practical advice and exercises designed specifically for Black women who want to break free from the chains of trauma and build a life they love.

This book is for Black women who are ready to reclaim their lives and heal their trauma. If you are ready to make lasting changes in your life, this book is for you. It is time for us to heal our trauma and step into our power, it is time for us to be unapologetically happy, it is time for us to wake up happy every day!

For too long, we have been told that we need to "just be strong" and that our feelings do not matter. But our feelings do matter. Our trauma does matter, and we deserve to finally heal from the pain that has been holding us back for far too long.

This book offers a step-by-step guide to help you:

- Understand what Black womanhood means in today's world
- Heal the traumas of your past
- Learn to love and accept yourself just as you are
- Create healthy relationships with others, and
- Build a life you love

From Trauma to Triumph is designed to be read in succession for the best outcome. It takes you through the stages of rebuilding your relationship with yourself so you can define and maintain healthy relationships with those around you.

Start by reading the introduction through Chapter 2, which will give you an overview of what self-care is and why it's so important for Black Women. Then, move on to Chapter 3, which is all about the power of your feminine energy. In this chapter, you'll learn how to use your feminine energy to heal yourself and create a life you love.

Then, in Chapter 4, you'll begin the process of healing from past trauma so that you are ready to lean in on Chapter 5 where you'll learn about loving yourself unconditionally and round out the chapter by writing a love letter to yourself as part of this healing process.

In Chapter 6, you'll learn about setting and maintaining healthy boundaries. This is an important part of self-care and healing because it allows you to create healthy relationships with others.

Chapter 7 is all about taking off the cape and breaking free from the Superwoman Myth. In this chapter, you'll learn that it's okay to ask for help and that you don't have to be perfect all the time.

Now that we have healed, learned to love ourselves, and learned how to set healthy boundaries, in Chapter 8 you'll take all your earlier learnings and apply them to finally break free from narcissistic and toxic relationships, both personally and professionally.

Finally, in Chapter 9, you'll learn about filling out your self-care toolkit. This includes a list of things you can do on a daily, weekly, or monthly basis to practice RADICAL self-care and additional resources you can look to for support on your journey.

After reading all the chapters, go back and review the conclusion to help solidify everything you've learned. Finally, take some time to reflect on what you've read and how you can apply the concepts in your own life. With the associated workbook, *Wake Up Happy, Sis: 90-Day Self-Care Challenge*, you will get activities and worksheets to help you create your own 90-day self-care journey to help you get started!

From Trauma To Triumph

The journey might not be easy, and it isn't always going to be fun or pretty, but it is so beautiful and worth it on the other side. Join me on the journey to your healing and wholeness, sis.

> *"If not this, then what? If not you, then who? If not now, then when?"*

I invite you to join me on this journey to healing and wholeness. Together, we can create a world where Black women are free to be their authentic selves. We can heal our trauma and build the lives we love. We can wake up happy every day!

If you are ready to take the first step on your journey to healing, this book is for you. Welcome home, sis. It's time to heal.

By LeAnne Dolce

Chapter 1

A Foundation in Self-Care

Self-care is the practice of taking care of oneself fully, physically, mentally, and emotionally. It is an important part of maintaining our overall health and wellbeing, and it helps us to take care of our thoughts and feelings. It's important to remember that self-care is not a one size fits all approach. What works for one person may not work for you. You need to find what works best for you, your needs at the time, and your unique circumstances.

Self-care is important for all women, but it is especially important for black women. Black women often carry a lot of stress and burdens, due to the many challenges we face in our lives. We often don't have the time or energy to take care of ourselves, because we are always taking care of everyone around us.

Self-care is crucial in maintaining our overall health and wellbeing. It helps us take care of our thoughts and feelings, and it allows us to make our wellness a priority in our lives. Self-care allows us to take a break from all the stress and responsibilities we deal with daily to focus on ourselves. When we are stressed out and exhausted, it can be difficult to think clearly or function properly. This is especially true for Black Women as we often are dealing with deep-rooted trauma, hurt, and anger, which can make it difficult to take care of ourselves properly.

Taking the time to relax and rejuvenate can help us to be more productive and effective when we return to our normal routine. Self-care can include anything from taking a relaxing bath to practicing yoga or meditation. It's important that you find something that works for you and that you enjoy doing. There is no "right" way to practice self-care, as long as you are taking care of yourself emotionally, mentally, spiritually, and physically.

Self-care is also digging deep into your emotional and mental states and healing from past traumas, releasing yourself from self-doubt, fear, guilt, worry, anxiety and toxicity. It isn't always pretty, but we must grow, heal, and love ourselves unconditionally.

It's also important to remember that self-care is not selfish. It's not always easy to make time for ourselves, but it's essential if we want to be healthy and happy. So, try not to feel guilty about taking some time for yourself. Instead, see it as an investment in your wellbeing. It's your golden ticket to being happy, healed, and whole.

If you're not sure where to start with self-care, then continue reading as I provide some tips on how to make self-care and wellness a priority in your life, how to heal from past trauma, and how to get rid of toxic and narcissistic relationships so you can love yourself unconditionally. You should also talk to your friends and family members about their self-care routines and see what works for them. And don't forget to ask your doctor or therapist for advice. They can offer guidance on how to take care of your mind, body, and soul using the 8 Dimensions of Self-Care.

Most importantly, remember that self-care is an ongoing process. It's not something you do once and then forget about. It's something you should make a part of your daily routine. By taking care of yourself, you'll be better able to take care of those around you. And that's something that we all need to do more of.

8 Dimensions of Self-Care

When I think about self-care as a primary component of our wellbeing, I like to look at it based on the 8 Dimensions of Self-Care: physical, emotional, intellectual, social, environmental, occupational, spiritual, and financial. Each dimension is important in its way, and they all work together to create a well-rounded life.

The 8 Dimensions of Self-Care are:
1. *Physical Self-Care* involves taking care of your body through exercise, sleep, proper nutrition, and getting regular medical check-ups. Regular body scans can help alert you to changes in your physical wellbeing.

2. *Emotional Self-Care* is about managing our emotions in a healthy way. It's about dealing with stress in a constructive

way, setting boundaries, and communicating our needs. It's about feeling good about ourselves and having a positive outlook on life.

3. *Intellectual Self-Care* aka Mental Health is about stimulating our minds and expanding our knowledge. It is about being able to think clearly and having good mental health habits, such as practicing meditation or mindfulness. It's about taking time to learn new things, challenging ourselves mentally, and engaging in creative thinking.

4. *Social Self-Care* is all about having fulfilling and supportive relationships with others. It's about having strong social connections and participating in activities that we enjoy. It's about feeling connected to others and having a sense of community; a sense of sisterhood.

5. *Environmental Self-Care* is about living in harmony with the environment. It's about being aware of the impact our actions have on the planet and taking steps to reduce our carbon footprint. It's also about taking care of the planet we live on and making sure that we are living in a sustainable way, such as by conserving resources and recycling.

6. ***Occupational Self-Care*** is having a career that you enjoy and that satisfies you. It's about finding meaning in your work and using your skills and talents to make a difference in the world. It also includes maintaining a healthy work-life balance.

7. ***Spiritual Self-Care*** relates to your sense of purpose and meaning in life. It is about connecting with something larger than ourselves and finding purpose in life. It's about developing a personal spirituality that works for you.

8. ***Financial Self-Care*** is about managing our money in a way that meets our needs and supports our lifestyle. It's about making smart financial decisions, planning for the future, and living within our means.

The 8 Dimensions of Self-Care are not mutually exclusive. In other words, you can experience wellbeing at different levels in more than one dimension at the same time. For example, you may be physically healthy but have low self-esteem or feel socially isolated. Or you may be financially successful but find no meaning or satisfaction in your work.

It's important to remember that each person's journey through the 8 Dimensions of Self-Care will be different. What matters most to you may not matter at all to someone else. And that's okay! There is no "right" or "wrong" way to think about wellness. As long as you are taking care of yourself across the 8 dimensions, you're doing it right.

When we have mastered self-care in each of these 8 dimensions, we create a life that is not only well-rounded but also fulfilling and satisfying. We are able to show up for ourselves and others in a way that is sustainable and nourishing.

The different types of self-care

Self-care comes in many different forms, and it's important to find what works best for you. Each person's approach to self-care will be different, but some general tips can be helpful for everyone.

1. Relaxation Techniques: This includes things like yoga, meditation, deep breathing exercises, and aromatherapy. These techniques can help to calm the mind and body and can be very relaxing.

2. Exercise: Exercise is a great way to release stress and tension, and it has many other benefits as well. It can help to improve mood, increase energy levels, and reduce stress levels.

3. Healthy Eating: Eating healthy foods helps the body to function at its best. It can boost energy levels, improve moods, and promote better sleep.

4. Socializing: Spending time with friends and family can help to reduce stress levels and promote positive emotions. It can also be a fun way to relax and enjoy yourself.

5. Self-Reflection: Taking time for introspection can be helpful in managing stress and improving self-awareness. Journaling, meditation, and walks in nature are all great ways to do this.

6. Pampering: Taking time for yourself to do things that you enjoy, like getting a massage or taking a bubble bath, can be a great way to relax and de-stress.

7. Creative Activities: Engaging in creative activities like painting, writing, dancing, or sculpting can be a great way to express yourself and relax your mind.

8. Service: Helping others can be a great way to promote feelings of happiness and satisfaction. Volunteering or simply lending a listening ear can make a big difference in someone's life.

Self-care is an important part of living a happy, healed, and whole life. By taking better care of yourself, you're showing your future self a love that has no bounds. So, make it a priority in your life today. Your future self will thank you for it.

How to stick with self-care in the long term

Self-care is essential for our overall well-being, but it can be difficult to stick with in the long term. Hell, sometimes life is just life, right? Well, here are a few tips for sticking with your new self-care routine for life.

1. Make sure that you set aside time each day for yourself and stick to it. This will help you to make self-care a habit.

If you need to schedule it into your day, block off your calendar and make it happen.

2. Try to find activities that you enjoy that invigorate your soul or that relax you, such as yoga, meditation, or reading.

3. Make sure that you are honest with yourself about your needs and limitations. Don't feel obligated to be superwoman for everyone; learn to say no when you need to.

4. Seek out supportive relationships with people who understand and appreciate your needs. They can hold space for you and hold you accountable for your new self-care lifestyle.

5. Be mindful of the way that you speak to yourself and work to replace negative self-talk with affirmations.

6. Take care of your physical health by eating nutritious foods and getting enough exercise.

7. Use the power of your feminine energy to nurture yourself and prioritize your own well-being.

8. Wake up every day happy and fulfilled, knowing that you have taken care of yourself in the best possible way.

Self-Care Just isn't for me... Why should I care?

If you think that self-care isn't for you or it is a luxury that you don't have access to, please think again. Self-care is for everyone, and it is not only beneficial to you, but it can also have a positive impact on your workplace and your close relationships. When people are happy and well-rounded, they are more productive and pleasant to be around.

Self-care has many benefits, including improved mental and physical health, reduced stress levels, and a stronger sense of self-awareness. When we take care of ourselves, we're able to function better both at work and at home. We're also less likely to experience anxiety and depression.

In addition to the mental and emotional benefits, self-care can also improve our physical health. When we make time for ourselves, we're more likely to exercise regularly, eat healthy foods, and get enough sleep. All these things lead to a stronger, healthier body.

Self-care is especially important for black women. We often put the needs of others before our own, and as a result, we can end up feeling overwhelmed and stressed out. Additionally, we may have trauma that makes us feel like we need to take care of others before taking care of ourselves.

Making self-care a priority can be hard, but it's worth it. We deserve to take care of ourselves, and when we do, we're better able to take care of those around us.

Self-care is about taking a break from the stresses of everyday life and focusing on yourself. It's about doing what works best for you, so experiment and find what activities make you feel relaxed and rejuvenated. There are no rules or regulations when it comes to self-care, so do what makes you happy and what helps you feel whole. By incorporating some of the basic principles of self-care into your life, you will start to see positive changes in your well-being.

While self-care is essential for maintaining your mental and physical health, it isn't always about overhauling your life all at one time. You can start small and work your way up. You don't need a lot of time or money to enjoy self-care activities, but you do have to be committed to making an investment in yourself.

What are you waiting for? Why not give it a try by incorporating some of the basic principles shared in this chapter and assessing your needs based on the 8 Dimensions of Self-Care? Where will you start?

Chapter 2

It's Time to Get Radical about Black Women's Self-Care

Did you know that only 2% of Black women say they practice self-care regularly, even though 78% say they feel a strong need to. (Source: National Black Women's Wellness Initiative)

This means that most Black women are not taking care of themselves, even though they know they need to. This is a huge problem. We are struggling and we are not taking the time to heal ourselves. We are putting everyone else's needs before our own and as a result, we are suffering.

By LeAnne Dolce

Self-care is vitally important for Black Women. We often take on the roles of mother, father, breadwinner, and caretaker for our families, as well as often being the emotional support for friends and loved ones. We rarely take time for ourselves, and when we do, we feel guilty. We think that if we're not doing everything for everyone, then we're not worthy of love.

Yes, Black women have been historically undervalued and unseen. We are often expected to be the "strong black woman" who never shows weakness. The foundation that never runs out of energy, love, or positivity for everyone else and who sacrifices all for her family and loved ones. This unrealistic expectation has led to us not taking care of ourselves mentally, emotionally, and sometimes not even physically.

We are the masters at putting the needs of others before our own; we feel like we must be Superwoman for everyone in our lives and put our own needs last. Indeed, we are constantly giving to others and not taking the time to nurture ourselves. This ultimately leads to burnout, resentment, and even depression. It causes us to feel guilty and anxious when we even THINK of doing something for ourselves. We walk around overwhelmed, stressed, and unappreciated. We must learn to love ourselves first and foremost so that we can teach others how to love us properly. It's important for us to take time for ourselves, to relax and recharge, so that we can show up happy, healthy, and whole in our own lives.

I bet you thought I was going to say that we should be taking time for ourselves so we can show up better in the lives of others. I certainly did not! I am saying the exact opposite. I am saying we need to get RADICAL about our self-care. We need and deserve to take time to focus on our self-care for our happiness and well-being. Because contrary to popular belief, it's not selfish to want to be happy, healed, and whole just for yourself and no one else's benefit. The outdated narrative that we must be happy, healed, and whole so that we can be better wives, parents, bosses, employees, etc. is just another part of the guilt and trauma that has been put upon us. I once believed it just like you probably do now. This narrative perpetuates the lie that the needs and happiness of others should always take priority and importance over our own; it tells us that our lives are only as important as the service we give to others and that line of thinking must stop!

By LeAnne Dolce

Sis, it's time for us to make a change. It's time for us to put ourselves first and take care of ourselves. We deserve to be happy and to feel fulfilled. We deserve to love ourselves as we nurture our bodies, minds, and souls.

I can hear you saying, now, wait a minute, LeAnne, back it up for a second. Did you just say we have to get RADICAL about our self-care? What do you even mean by that? Yes, I said it and I meant it! I mean that we have to take a more active and hands-on approach to our self-care and wellness. And when I say RADICAL, I mean looking at self-care through a different lens; a more holistic and healing lens that takes our whole person into account.

Self-care isn't just about taking a walk or getting a massage or having a relaxing bath with a glass of wine. Yes, all those things are self-care acts, but there is so much more to self-care than the pretty and fun things. Self-care is also about taking control of all aspects of your self-care and letting go of the guilt and anxiety associated with your current lack of self-care.

In my Signature RADICAL Self-care Blueprint (TM), I define RADICAL as a set of principles for how we govern ourselves concerning our self-care and wellness practices.

- **Release:** We commit to releasing ourselves from the guilt and trauma of putting everyone else's needs before our own. We also release the need to people please and be everything to everyone.
- **Acknowledge:** We acknowledge that we are worthy of love, happiness, and relaxation just for ourselves with no strings attached.
- **Declutter:** To design a life that we love, we must declutter our minds, bodies, and spirits of anything that does not serve us or make us happy. This includes toxic relationships, negative self-talk, and any unhealthy habits so that we can design a life we love! We deserve to live a life that is fulfilling, stress-free, and full of joy. We also declutter our schedule by delegating and automating tasks and responsibilities to free up time for ourselves.
- **Invest:** We invest in ourselves by making our well-being a priority. This includes investing time, energy, and money into activities, experiences, and people that make us happy and help us to relax and

recharge. We create a self-care plan that works for us as individuals.

- **Connect:** We will connect with trustworthy people who hold space for us and can help us. These people can be friends, family, therapists, or even a support group.
- **Attentive:** Be Attentive to your needs and make sure to schedule time for yourself. This can be as simple as taking a break to walk outside or having a relaxing bath with a glass of wine. It can also mean meeting with your support group weekly. You can do a body scan to help you determine what you need at this moment.
- **Love:** Love who we are through our healing and growth journey. There will be times when it is hard, ugly, and painful, but WHEN you make it to the other side, it will be so beautiful and worth all the effort. So, remember to love yourself and give yourself grace as you walk this journey of healing and growth.

"Radical self-care for black women means taking active steps to improve our well-being without guilt or anxiety. It means

> acknowledging that we are worthy of love and happiness, and investing time, energy, and money into activities, experiences, and people that make us happy. It means creating a self-care plan that works for us as individuals. And it means taking care of ourselves so we can show up better for ourselves."
>
> *-Leanne Betasamosake Simpson*

Sometimes we are reluctant to take time for ourselves because we feel like we're abandoning our families. We think our family can't succeed without us; as if everything will fall apart if we aren't there to personally oversee it. This is simply not true. Our families will be just fine without us as we take a well-deserved break. In fact, they may even benefit from our absence, as it will allow them to learn how to do it for themselves. This is an important life lesson that we all must learn.

We must show up for ourselves FIRST before we can ever think of showing up for anyone else. Yes, it is ok to do for yourself without it being for the benefit of others. Yes, it is absolutely ok to want to wake up happy and show up for

By LeAnne Dolce

ourselves before others. When we make time for ourselves, we are allowing ourselves to be the best possible versions of ourselves. Why wouldn't we love and care for ourselves, just as much as we love and care for our families and friends? When we take care of and show love to ourselves, everyone around us benefits because love attracts love. So, let's start taking care of ourselves so that we can continue to be the strong and amazing women that we are!

Tips for practicing RADICAL self-care

There are many ways to add self-care to your life. For example, you can wake up a few minutes earlier each morning to take a walk or do some Yoga. You can also take a break from work in the afternoon to read your favorite book. If you're feeling overwhelmed and stressed, take some time for yourself. This may mean taking a break from work, canceling social engagements, or spending more time at home. Finally, don't be afraid to ask for help when you need it. There are people who love and support you, and they want to see you succeed.

So, what are some ways that Black Women can practice self-care? Below are just a few suggestions:

1. **Get enough sleep:** This is one of the most important things we can do for ourselves. Most adults need around eight hours of sleep per night, but sometimes we need more or less depending on how our bodies are feeling. Make sure you're getting enough rest so that you can function at your best.
2. **Practice gratitude:** One way to instantly boost your mood is by practicing gratitude. Every day, take a few minutes to write down three things that you're grateful for. This could be anything from the sun shining to your favorite pair of shoes. When we focus on what's good in our lives, it's easier to let go of the negative thoughts that bring us down.
3. **Meditate:** Meditation is a great way to calm the mind and ease anxiety. It's also been shown to improve sleep, concentration, and overall well-being. If you're new to meditation, there are plenty of guided meditations available online or on apps like Headspace. These are just a few ideas to get you started on your self-care journey. The most important thing is to find what works for you and make self-care a priority in your life. When we take care of ourselves, we are better equipped to take care of

those around us. So, let's love ourselves enough to put our well-being first!

4. **Take breaks:** When we're feeling overwhelmed or stressed, it's important to take a step back and take a break. This can mean taking a few minutes to yourself to relax and rejuvenate, or it could mean taking a vacation from your responsibilities. Either way, taking some time for yourself will do wonders for your mental and emotional health.

5. **Exercise:** Wake up a few minutes earlier than usual so you can take a nice walk or do some yoga. Exercise releases endorphins, which have mood-boosting and stress-reducing effects. Taking a brisk walk, going for a run, or even just doing some simple stretches at home can make a world of difference.

6. **Seek professional help:** If you're struggling with depression, anxiety, or any other mental health issue, seeking professional help is always a good idea. Traditionally, this has been taboo in many Black families, but we are here to remove the negative stigma associated with mental health. A therapist can provide you with the tools and support you need to manage your mental health healthily and productively.

7. **Find a supportive sisterhood community:** It's important to surround yourself with supportive and positive people who will encourage your healing journey. There are many online and offline communities for black women to connect with one another, such as my community, The Sister Circle. The Sister Circle provides support, advice, and friendship. It is also a great resource for wellness training and self-development tools.

Benefits of self-care for Black Women

Self-care has many benefits for Black Women, including improved mental and emotional health, increased self-esteem and confidence, and improved physical health. Self-care is an act of self-love. It is an acknowledgment of our worthiness and a commitment to taking care of ourselves, mind, body, and soul. When we make our self-care a priority, we are better able to show up for ourselves and then show up for those around us. We can also heal from the trauma of our past and move forward in our lives with confidence and authenticity.

By LeAnne Dolce

When we make our self-care a priority, we show up happier, healthier, and more whole in our lives. We are better able to set and maintain healthy boundaries, which is important in both personal and professional relationships. We can show ourselves unconditional love and we can start the healing process from the trauma of our past. And when we are healed, we can fully walk in our feminine energy, and we can move forward in our lives with confidence and authenticity.

Black women often bear the brunt of emotional labor in their families and communities. Self-care is a way for black women to recharge and take a break from the stress of daily life. It can help black women manage their emotions, which can lead to improved mental health. Black women who engage in self-care are more likely to have better relationships with others. Self-care can also improve productivity and creativity. Finally, self-care can help black women connect with their inner selves, leading to a greater sense of peace and calm. Sis, it's time to get RADICAL about our self-care! We have been putting everyone else's needs before our own for far too long. It's time to take control of our self-care and make our well-being a priority. When we make our self-care a priority, we show up happier, healthier, and more whole in our lives. We are better able to set and maintain healthy boundaries, which is important in both personal and professional relationships. We can show ourselves unconditional love and we can start the healing process from the trauma of our past. And when we are healed, we can fully walk in our feminine energy, and we can move forward in our lives with confidence and authenticity.

When we take care of ourselves, we are better able to show up for others healthily and happily. So let's release the guilt, acknowledge our worthiness, declutter our minds and bodies, invest in ourselves, and create a self-care plan that works for us. It's time for us to design the lives we love!

> *"Self-care is not selfish. You cannot serve from an empty vessel."*
> ***-Elaine Heath***

By LeAnne Dolce

Chapter 3

Harnessing the Power of Your Feminine Energy

In order to harness the power of your feminine energy, you must first understand what it is and how it works. In essence, feminine energy is creative, intuitive, and expressive. It is the force that motivates us to connect with others and to create meaningful lives. When we tap into our feminine energy, we can access our intuition and creativity, which allows us to move through life with greater ease and grace.

Feminine energy is often misunderstood and even feared by those who are not familiar with it.

From Trauma To Triumph

This is because feminine energy is so different from the masculine energy that dominates our world. While masculine energy is focused on action and achieving goals, feminine energy is about flow and receptivity. This can be confusing for people who are used to operating from a place of linear thinking and concrete goal setting. However, when we embrace our feminine energy, we open ourselves up to a world of possibilities. We can connect with ourselves and others on a deeper level and create more meaningful lives.

So how can you harness the power of your feminine energy? We must clear away the blocks that are preventing us from accessing this powerful force within ourselves. In this chapter, we will explore some of the most common blocks and how to release them. This will allow you to tap into your feminine power so that you can create the life you desire.

If you're ready to harness the power of your feminine energy, then keep reading. By the end of this chapter, you will have everything you need to start tapping into your feminine power. Let's get started!

What is Feminine Energy?

Feminine energy is the creative, intuitive, and emotional energy that is within all of us. It is the energy that allows us to connect with our creativity, our intuition, and our emotions. When we connect with our feminine energy, we allow ourselves to be more open, expressive, and vulnerable. We also become more receptive to the guidance of our intuition.

Feminine energy is often seen as being in opposition to masculine energy. This is because masculine energy is generally seen as being more rational, logical, and goal oriented. However, it is important to remember that we all have both masculine and feminine energy within us. And it is when these two energies are in balance that we can create the lives we desire.

Stop Blocking Your Feminine Energy

One of the most common ways that people block their feminine energy is by trying to control everything. When we try to control everything, we are not allowing ourselves to flow with life. We are holding onto our power so tightly that we are preventing ourselves from accessing our intuition and creativity. This can lead to feelings of frustration, overwhelm, and even depression.

If you find yourself trying to control everything, it's time to let go and allow yourself to flow with life. Trust that the universe has a plan for you and know that you are being guided every step of the way. When you let go of control, you open yourself up to new possibilities and experiences. You may even find that things start to flow more easily in your life.

Another way people block their feminine energy is by trying to be perfect. When we strive for perfection, we are holding ourselves back from being our authentic selves. We are afraid to make mistakes and so we limit ourselves in what we do and how we express ourselves. This can lead to feelings of shame, unworthiness, and inadequacy.

If you find yourself striving for perfection, it's time to let go of that need. Embrace your imperfections and know that they are what make you unique and special. When you let go of the need to be perfect, you allow yourself to be more authentic and you open yourself up to new possibilities.

Another way people block their feminine energy is by numbing themselves. This can be done in many ways, such as using food, alcohol, drugs, or shopping, to name a few. When we numb ourselves, we are not allowing ourselves to feel our emotions. We are running away from our pain instead of facing it. This can lead to feelings of disconnection, loneliness, and emptiness.

If you find yourself numbing yourself, it's time to face your pain. Allow yourself to feel your emotions and know that they are here to guide you. When you allow yourself to feel your pain, you open yourself up to healing and transformation.

Another way people block their feminine energy is through the limiting beliefs that they carry. If you find yourself believing any of these things, it's time to let go of those beliefs and embrace your power. You are worthy of love, success, and abundance. Trust that you have everything you need to create the life you desire. Some limiting beliefs include:

- **Fear:** We may be afraid of being seen as weak or powerless if we allow ourselves to be open and vulnerable. We may also be afraid of being rejected or judged if we express our emotions.

- **Shame:** We may feel like we are not good enough or that we have to be perfect. We may also feel like we are not worthy of love and connection.
- **Doubt:** We may doubt our ability to be successful if we follow our intuition instead of our logical mind. We may also doubt our worthiness of love and abundance.
- **Lack of confidence:** We may doubt our ability to be successful or attract what we desire.
- **Negative self-talk:** We may tell ourselves that we are not good enough or that we will never be successful.

Finally, people block their feminine energy by disconnecting from their bodies, emotions, or intuition. This can be done in many ways, such as not listening to our bodily cues, numbing our sensations, or dissociating from our physical form. We may also feel disconnected from other people or the natural world. When we disconnect from our bodies, we are not allowing ourselves to fully experience life. This can lead to feelings of disconnection, loneliness, and isolation.

If you find yourself disconnecting from your body, it's time to reconnect. Allow yourself to feel your emotions and sensations. Listen to your body's cues and trust that it is here to guide you. When you reconnect with your body, you open yourself up to new possibilities and experiences.

Deciding to connect with your feminine energy is the first step on the journey to balance. By making this decision, you are opening yourself up to a world of possibilities. Trust that you are being guided and supported every step of the way. Allow yourself to flow with life and know that you are worthy of love, joy, and abundance.

Start by deciding to connect with your feminine energy. From there, allow yourself to flow with life and trust that you are being supported every step of the way.

If you're ready to release the blocks that are holding you back from accessing your feminine energy, then keep reading. In the next section, we will explore some of the most effective ways to do this.

Releasing the blocks that hold you back
There are many effective ways to release the blocks that are holding you back from accessing your feminine energy. Some of the most effective ways to do this are:

- **Meditation:** One of the most effective ways to release the blocks that are holding you back from accessing your feminine energy is through meditation. Meditation allows us to quiet our minds and connect with our innermost thoughts and feelings. When we meditate, we can connect with our intuition and guidance.
- **Journaling:** Another effective way to release the blocks that are holding you back from accessing your feminine energy is through journaling. Journaling allows us to express our thoughts and feelings in a safe and non-judgmental space. It also allows us to track our progress and growth.
- **Visualization:** Another effective way to release the blocks that are holding you back from accessing your feminine energy is through visualization. Visualization allows us to see ourselves in the life we desire. It also allows us to tap into our creative power and manifest our desires.

- **Affirmations:** Another effective way to release the blocks that are holding you back from accessing your feminine energy is through affirmations. Affirmations are positive statements that we repeat to ourselves. They help to reprogram our subconscious mind and attract our desires.
- **Breath work:** Another effective way to release the blocks that are holding you back from accessing your feminine energy is through breath work. Breath work helps us to release stress and tension from our bodies. It also helps us to connect with our innermost thoughts and feelings.

No matter which method you choose, the most important thing is that you commit to releasing the blocks that are holding you back from accessing your feminine energy. When you do this, you open yourself up to limitless possibilities.

Start your journey to accessing your feminine energy today. Choose one of the methods listed below and commit to releasing the blocks that are holding you back. As you do this, you will notice a shift in your life. You will start to feel more connected to your intuition and guidance. You will also start to attract your desires with ease. Most importantly, you will begin to feel happier and more fulfilled. So, what are you waiting for? Start your journey today!

Tapping into Your Feminine Energy

Now that you have released those blocks, it's time to start tapping into your feminine power. Here are some ways to get started:

1. **Get in touch with your emotions:** One of the best ways to tap into your feminine energy is to get in touch with your emotions. Allow yourself to feel your emotions fully and healthily express them.
2. **Connect with your intuition:** Another great way to tap into your feminine energy is to connect with your intuition. Start paying attention to the guidance you receive from your intuition and act on it.
3. **Be open and vulnerable:** Another way to tap into your feminine energy is to be open and vulnerable. Allow yourself to be seen and heard. Express your emotions and thoughts freely.
4. **Nurture yourself:** Another great way to tap into your feminine energy is to nurture yourself. Give

yourself the time and space to relax and rejuvenate. Take care of your body and mind.

5. **Connect with nature:** Another great way to tap into your feminine energy is to connect with nature. Spend time in nature and allow yourself to be nourished by the Earth.

6. **Be creative:** Another great way to tap into your feminine energy is to be creative. Express yourself through art, music, dance, or any other creative outlet.

7. **Be loving and kind:** Another great way to tap into your feminine energy is to be loving and kind. Show love and compassion to yourself and others.

8. **Choose love:** Another great way to tap into your feminine energy is to choose love. No matter what life throws your way, choose to respond with love.

9. **Forgive yourself:** Another great way to tap into your feminine energy is to forgive yourself. We all make mistakes. Learn from them and then let them go.

10. **Heal your wounds:** Another great way to tap into your feminine energy is to heal your wounds. If you have any unresolved pain or trauma, now is the time to heal it. When you heal your wounds, you open yourself up to more love and abundance.

When you tap into the power of your feminine energy, you will find that you are better able to achieve your goals and live a life that is in alignment with your true desires. When you connect with your feminine energy, you become more creative and intuitive. You are better able to see the possibilities that exist for you and to create a life that is in harmony with your deepest desires.

How feminine energy can help you heal past trauma
When you connect with your feminine energy, you will find that you are better able to heal past trauma. This is because feminine energy is all about healing and restoration. When you connect with your feminine energy, you allow yourself to move through the healing process in a more relaxed and open manner. You also become more receptive to the messages that your intuition is sending you.

If you are struggling with past trauma, it can be helpful to connect with your feminine energy. This may involve practicing meditation or journaling, or it may involve working with a therapist who understands the power of feminine energy. When you connect with your feminine energy, you allow yourself to heal more holistically and authentically. You also allow yourself to tap into the power of your intuition and connect with your inner wisdom.

The bottom line is that when you connect with your feminine energy, you become better able to achieve your goals and live a life that is in alignment with your true desires. You also become more creative, intuitive, and expressive.

So, if you're ready to start experiencing the benefits of using your feminine energy to heal, then take a look at the blocks that may be preventing you from doing so and start working on releasing them. It won't be easy, but it will be worth it in the end. Just remember that there is no one-size-fits-all approach when it comes to connecting with your feminine energy, you have to find what works best for you and go with that.

Chapter 4

Healing From Past Trauma

Black women often bear the brunt of emotional, mental, and other pain inflicted upon them throughout their lives. Whether from family, friends, or society at large, this trauma can take its toll and lead to a feeling of being overwhelmed, depressed, and stressed. This trauma stops us from being able to move forward and create the life we want for ourselves.

This chapter is devoted to helping us heal from our trauma so we can start living our best life on our terms. We start by understanding just what trauma is and how it affects us. We will explore ways to deal with the pain, anger, and hurt that trauma can cause so that we can move on and create healthy boundaries, release ourselves from toxic and narcissistic relationships, and finally learn how to love ourselves again after trauma has tried to break us down.

By the end of this chapter, you will have the tools you need to start the healing process and begin moving forward toward the life you deserve.

What is trauma?

Trauma is defined as a deeply distressing or disturbing experience. It can be physical, emotional, mental, or spiritual. Trauma can be caused by those who want to hurt us, but it can also be caused by well-intentioned parents and other influential people in our lives. This trauma can have a profound and lasting effect on an individual, often leading to feelings of anxiety, depression, worthlessness, and isolation. And no two people will experience, process, and be affected by trauma in the same way.

For Black women, past trauma is often compounded by the everyday stressors of racism, sexism, and classism. This can lead to feelings of being overwhelmed, stressed, and struggling to love ourselves. Black women must make self-care a priority in their lives and use the power of our feminine energy to heal themselves from trauma, hurt, and pain.

There are many signs that someone is struggling with past trauma. They may have difficulty sleeping, experience anxiety or mood swings, feel disconnected from others, or engage in self-destructive behaviors. They may also have trouble maintaining healthy relationships, struggle to trust people, and have a hard time moving on from the past. If you are experiencing any of these signs, it is important to seek help from a therapist or counselor who can assist you in dealing with your trauma.

Healing from trauma

The first step in healing from trauma is acknowledging that it has occurred. This can be difficult, as we may want to forget about the pain and hurt that we have experienced. We may also have suppressed our memories of the trauma to cope with it. However, denying that the trauma occurred will only prevent us from healing and moving on.

By LeAnne Dolce

Once we have acknowledged the trauma, it is crucial to face our trauma head-on if we want to begin the healing process. We need to start working through the emotions that come with trauma. This may include talking about our experiences with a therapist or counselor, writing about them in a journal, or participating in group therapy. It is important to release the emotions associated with the trauma so that we can begin to heal. This process can take time, but it is essential to our well-being. It is also important, during this time, to take care of our physical well-being by eating healthy, exercising, and getting enough sleep.

It is also important to create healthy boundaries in our lives after the trauma. We may need to distance ourselves from people who trigger our trauma, set limits on what we are willing to do or share with others, and learn how to say no when we are feeling overwhelmed. Creating these boundaries will help us protect ourselves from further hurt and pain.

We also need to do some soul-searching to forgive those who have hurt us. This can be a difficult process, but it is necessary for healing. Just how do we forgive someone who has caused us so much pain? It doesn't happen overnight, that's for sure. But, bit by bit, we can start to let go of the anger and hurt that they have caused us.

A great way to begin the process of forgiveness is to write a letter to the person (or people) who have hurt you. In this letter, express your anger, pain, and hurt. Be honest and tell them how they hurt you and how you feel about it. Get it all out and I mean ALL OUT! Once you have done this, imagine forgiving them in your mind and working your way up to speaking it out of your mouth. It may take some time before you can say it and mean it, but it will come, trust the process. This doesn't mean that what they did was okay, but it does mean that you are ready to move on with your life. Even if you never send it or speak to them again, this process will help YOU let go of the trauma. Forgiveness is for you, not them.

When you hold on to trauma, it prevents you from loving, living, and trusting with your whole heart. You can't live your best life when you constantly feel anxious, stressed, and disconnected from others. Forgiveness is how you take back your power. You are choosing to move on and live your life to the fullest.

By LeAnne Dolce

Finally, we need to learn how to love ourselves again. This may be the most difficult task of all, but it is essential to our healing. We are constantly bombarded with messages that tell us we are not good enough and we internalize these messages and even begin to believe them. Too often, we focus on forgiving others while forgetting to forgive ourselves. We berate ourselves for our mistakes, beat ourselves up for not being perfect, and compare ourselves to others who seem to have it all together. But to heal from trauma, we need to learn how to love and accept ourselves just as we are because healing begins with self-love.

One of the most important things we can do for ourselves after trauma is to learn how to love and appreciate our bodies, minds, and spirits. This can be a difficult task, especially if we have been told that we are not good enough or that we are not worthy of love. However, it is essential to our healing. Learning to love ourselves again is a process, but it starts with making self-care a priority. It means listening to our needs and honoring them. It means surrounding ourselves with people who support and love us. And it means forgiving ourselves for our mistakes, and shortcomings, and for the feeling that we somehow caused our trauma.

We need to start by accepting ourselves exactly as we are. This means accepting our flaws and imperfections. It also means recognizing our strengths and accomplishments. We need to forgive ourselves for any mistakes we have made in the past and focus on the present moment.

We can also practice self-care activities such as exercise, meditation, journaling, and spending time in nature. These activities help to reduce stress, improve our mood, and increase our overall sense of well-being. When we make self-care a priority, we are sending a message to ourselves that we are worthy of love and care. Remember, making self-care a priority is an act of self-love. It is an investment in YOU!

To heal from past trauma, it is important to understand that you are not alone. Many other black women have experienced similar pain and have gone on to live happily and fulfilled lives.

Another way to heal from past trauma is by using the power of your feminine energy. Black women have long been considered the backbone of the family and community. We are often the ones who are expected to be strong and never show weakness. However, this expectation can often lead to us repressing our emotions, which can eventually lead to pain and suffering.

Instead of repressing your emotions, try to embrace them. Allow yourself to feel anger, sadness, and pain. These emotions are a part of who you are, and they do not make you weak. By allowing yourself to feel them, you will begin the healing process and start moving forward with your life. Feel the feelings when they come, but do not allow them to take over your life and swallow you whole. You have to fight to conquer them and get back to being happy. Healing comes in those moments of fighting!

The effects of past trauma can be devastating and often prevent Black women from living their best lives. Many carry the weight of pain and hurt inflicted on them throughout their lives. This can manifest in many ways, including feelings of inadequacy, overwhelm, and stress. It is essential that Black women learn how to heal themselves to move forward in life with happiness and peace. This can be a difficult task, but it is possible with self-care and the use of healing modalities. Only when Black women heal themselves will they be able to show up in the world happy, healed, and whole.

6 tips for healing from past trauma

Black women must seek out resources that can help them heal from their past trauma. When Black women heal themselves, they can shine brightly in a world that often does not appreciate them. Healing is possible and Black women are strong enough to achieve it. Here are 5 tips for healing from past trauma.

1. **Forgive yourself and others** - Healing begins with forgiveness. Forgive yourself for what has happened and forgive those who have hurt you. Don't dwell on the past, focus on the present moment. This will help you to be more mindful and appreciate the good moments in your life.
2. **Seek professional help if you are struggling to cope with your trauma**. A therapist can help you work through your emotions and start the healing

process. Commit to healing, even when the going gets tough. Healing takes time, but it is worth the effort involved. Focus on the present moment and appreciate the good moments in your life. This will help you to move on from the past.

3. **Read self-help books or listen to podcasts that focus on healing from trauma**. These resources can provide valuable information and support. When Black women heal themselves, they can shine brightly in a world that often does not appreciate them. Healing is possible and Black women are strong enough to achieve it.

4. **Connect with other Black women who are working to heal their trauma**. This can provide a sense of sisterhood, connection, and support. This can provide a sense of connection and support. Many Black women have overcome their trauma and gone on to lead happy and fulfilling lives. You can too. Many online communities offer support and resources for healing from trauma. These communities can provide a sense of connection and support. They can also offer valuable information and resources. Find a support system - A supportive network of friends and family can make a world of

difference. They can provide you with emotional support and practical assistance when needed.

5. **Make a commitment to your healing.** Healing takes time, but it is possible with dedication and hard work. Commit to healing - Healing takes time and commitment. Be patient with yourself and stick with it even when the going gets tough.

6. **Be patient with yourself**. Healing is a process, not an event. Allow yourself the time and space to heal at your own pace. Making self-care a priority is essential for healing from past trauma. When you take care of yourself, you are better able to navigate the world with strength and confidence. Black women are often expected to be superwomen and sacrifice their own needs to meet the needs of others. This can result in feelings of resentment and frustration.

Black women oftentimes carry the burden of trauma from past experiences. This can take a toll on their mental and emotional health. If you are a Black woman struggling to heal from past trauma, know that you are not alone. Healing from trauma is possible, but it requires time, patience, and dedication. There are many resources available to help black women heal, including therapists, self-help books or podcasts, and online communities like *The Sister Circle*. It is important for black women to connect with other women who are also working to heal their trauma. This can provide support and connection. Black women are strong enough to heal their trauma and shine brightly in a world that often does not appreciate them.

Chapter 5

Healthy Boundaries as Healing Agents

It can be difficult to set and maintain healthy boundaries in personal and professional relationships. Many people struggle with saying no, setting limits, and standing up for themselves. This is especially true for those who have a history of trauma or abuse.

When you don't have healthy boundaries, you may find yourself overwhelmed and stressed out. You may also find yourself in toxic or narcissistic relationships where you are not appreciated or supported, instead you are berated, belittled, and even physically abused.

By LeAnne Dolce

It is important to learn how to set and maintain healthy boundaries to protect yourself emotionally, spiritually, physically, and mentally. By doing so, you will be able to wake up happy every day and show up healed and whole in life. Setting and maintaining healthy boundaries is an essential part of any healing journey. When you have healthy boundaries, you can take care of yourself and your needs.

If you have a history of trauma or abuse, it can be difficult to set and maintain healthy boundaries. This is because you may not feel safe or comfortable doing so. But it is important to learn how to set and maintain healthy boundaries so you will be able to take care of yourself in a healthier way and get rid of the relationships that are no longer serving you.

What are healthy boundaries?

Boundaries are the limits we set to protect ourselves. They are the lines we draw that define what is and is not acceptable to us. They help us to know where we end, and others begin. Healthy boundaries are important because they help us to take care of ourselves. When we have healthy boundaries, we can say no to things that are not good for us. We are also able to set limits on what we will tolerate from others. And we can stand up for ourselves when needed.

Different people have different boundaries, which are influenced by culture, personality, and the social context in which they live. For example, some people are comfortable with hugging and physical touch, while others are not. Some people are okay with profanity, while others are not. What is acceptable in a personal situation may not be acceptable in a work environment; you wouldn't speak to your boss in the same way you speak to your spouse or good friends. It is important to respect other people's boundaries as well as your own.

Some examples of healthy boundaries include:
- Telling people how you want to be communicated with, whether that be through email, text, or in person
- Setting limits on how much time you spend with someone or how often you see them
- Establishing rules and regulations for how you will be treated in a relationship
- Requiring respect for your physical space and personal belongings

- Having clear communication about sex and sexual boundaries
- Asking for what you want and need from others
- Saying no when you don't want to do something
- Stating your opinions and beliefs even if they are different from others

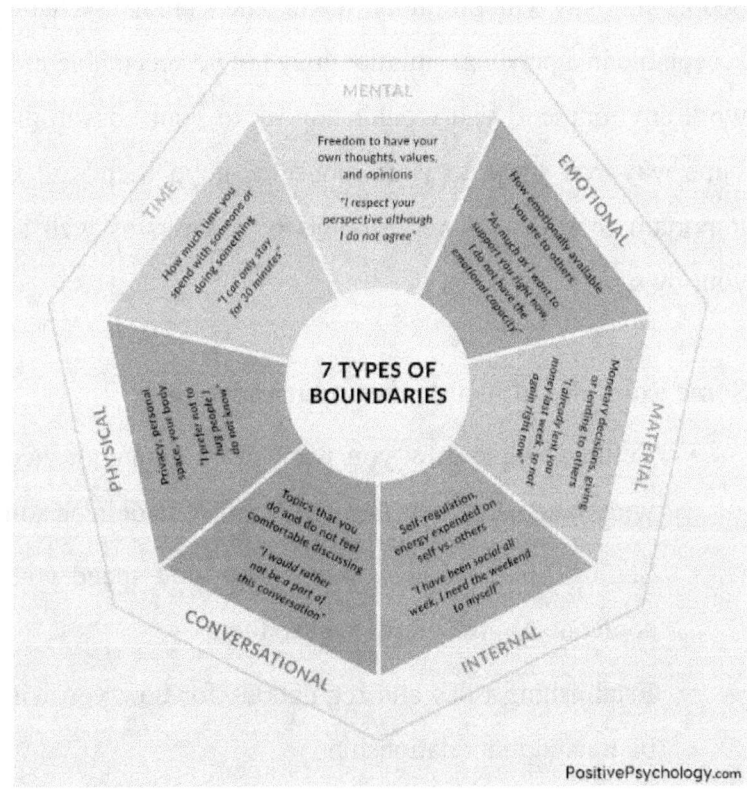

Positive Psychology lists the 7 Types of Boundaries as:

- **Mental Boundaries:** Defining your thoughts, values, and beliefs. Deciding what information you will allow into your mind and not allowing others to control or manipulate your thoughts.
- **Emotional Boundaries:** Understanding how emotionally available you are to others.
- **Physical Boundaries:** Defining your physical limits, privacy, and personal space. Respecting your body and people's access to it. Not allowing others to physically hurt or abuse you.
- **Time Boundaries:** Setting limits on how much time you spend with others or on certain activities. Having time for yourself to rest, relax and do things you enjoy. Not allowing others to control or monopolize your time.
- **Conversational Boundaries:** Deciding what topics are off-limits and ending conversations that make you feel uncomfortable.
- **Internal Boundaries:** Self-regulating the energy expended on yourself and others and knowing what you need to do to recharge and renew yourself.

- **Material Boundaries:** These are the limits we set around our possessions and resources. Deciding what you are and are not comfortable with in terms of possessions and setting limits on how much money or credit you will use and/ or lend.

How can you tell if you need to set a boundary?

There are a few key indicators that you may need to set a boundary with someone in your life. Assess how you are feeling based on the 7 types of boundaries. If you find yourself feeling overwhelmed or stressed out in any area, this is a sign that you need to set a boundary. If you are in a toxic or narcissistic relationship, this is another indicator that you need to set a boundary.

Healthy boundaries are important because they help you to protect yourself emotionally and mentally, and they also help you to take care of yourself in a healthier way. If you have a history of trauma or abuse, it can be difficult to set and maintain healthy boundaries. This is because you may not feel safe or comfortable doing so. You may also find yourself in toxic or narcissistic relationships where you are not appreciated or supported.

How to set healthy boundaries

There are a few key ways that you can set healthy boundaries. The first step is to identify your needs and what you are comfortable with.

It is also important to be aware of your body language and tone of voice when setting boundaries, this can help the other person to understand that you are serious about setting a boundary.

Once you have set a boundary, it is important to stick to it. This may mean saying no or walking away from a situation that makes you feel uncomfortable.

Advantages of Healthy Boundaries

There are a lot of advantages to setting and maintaining healthy boundaries, including:

1. Healthy boundaries help you to take care of yourself emotionally, spiritually, physically, and mentally.
2. They help you to set limits on what you will tolerate from others.
3. They help you to stand up for yourself when needed.
4. They help you to define who you are and what is important to you.

5. They help you to maintain your independence and integrity.

6. They help you to have healthier relationships with others.

7. They help you to feel safe and in control.

8. They help you to feel empowered and strong.

9. They allow you to be your authentic self without judgment or criticism from others.

10. They create a sense of peace and calmness in your life."

How to set and maintain healthy boundaries

There are a few things you can do to set and maintain healthy boundaries.

First, it is important to remember that you have a right to set and maintain healthy boundaries. No one has the right to cross your boundaries without your consent. If someone does cross your boundaries, you have the right to assertively tell them to stop.

Second, you must be clear about your needs and what you are comfortable with. You need to be able to communicate your needs clearly and assertively. It is important to be assertive when setting boundaries and to use "I" statements. For example, you could say, "I need some time to myself" or "I don't feel comfortable talking about that right now." This ensures that the other person knows what your limits are. It is also important to be aware of your triggers and what makes you feel uncomfortable. This will help you know when someone is crossing your boundaries.

Third, recognize when you need to set physical boundaries to protect yourself. This could mean creating some space between you and the other person, or it could mean saying no to certain activities or situations. Keeping yourself safe is always a priority.

Fourth, look to heal past trauma that is causing you to back away from the boundaries you have set. This can be done through therapy, journaling, and other self-care practices. This includes taking care of yourself emotionally, physically, and mentally. When you take care of yourself, you will be better at sticking to your boundaries.

Finally, it is important to surround yourself with people who respect your boundaries. These people can provide you with emotional and mental support. They will support you and make sure you are comfortable. They will also be more likely to respect your boundaries themselves.

If someone crosses your boundaries, it is important to assertively tell them to stop. You have a right to protect yourself and to set the limits that are best for you. If the person does not respect your boundaries, it may be necessary to end the relationship.

Maintaining healthy boundaries is essential for preserving your mental and emotional health. It can be difficult to do, but with practice and the right tools, you can protect yourself from boundary crossings and narcissistic relationships. When you surround yourself with people who respect your boundaries, you will find it easier to stick to them. And finally, don't forget to practice self-care. This includes taking care of yourself emotionally and mentally. When you take care of yourself, you will be better able to cope with boundary crossings and maintain healthy boundaries.

Chapter 6

The Gift of Unconditional Self-Love

Now that we have learned how to tap into the power of our feminine energy, started healing from our past traumas, and set healthy boundaries, the next stop on our self-care journey is unconditional self-love. Often, we are our own worst critics and don't give ourselves the love that we deserve. This chapter provides tips on how to incorporate self-love into your life, as well as a guide on how to write a love letter to yourself. Healing from trauma is an important part of this process, and this chapter provides insight into why self-love is so crucial for Black Women.

By LeAnne Dolce

What is unconditional love, and why is it so important for Black Women?

Unconditional love is love that is not based on any condition or expectation. It is pure, and it is the foundation for a healthy relationship with yourself or others. For Black Women, it is especially important to learn how to give and receive unconditional love, as we often carry a lot of trauma and pain. Trauma can prevent us from fully loving ourselves and others, which is why it is crucial to begin the healing process with unconditional self-love. Healing allows us to connect with our authentic selves, find strength in our ability to be vulnerable, and experience true happiness and joy. When we can love ourselves unconditionally, we can also give and receive that same love from others. This creates a foundation of love and support that is crucial for Black Women.

Now that we know what unconditional self-love is, let's talk about what it isn't. Unconditional self-love is not selfish, it is not narcissistic, and it is not self-indulgent. It isn't thinking that we are perfect and above reproach, it isn't thinking that everyone should love and adore us, it isn't boastful or proud, but It is simply the act of giving yourself the love and care that you deserve, without any expectations or conditions. When you love yourself unconditionally, you are committing to your own happiness and well-being. This doesn't mean that you will never experience pain or struggle again, but it does mean that you will always be there for yourself, no matter what.

Here are some tips on how to start incorporating unconditional self-love into your life:

1. Forgive yourself: We all make mistakes, and we all have things in our past that we aren't proud of. Forgiving yourself is an important part of the self-love process. It allows you to let go of the pain and hurt that you may be holding onto, and it allows you to move forward with your life.

2. Be gentle with yourself: We are often our own worst critics, and we can be very hard on ourselves. Learning to be gentle with yourself is a crucial part of self-love. It means being kind and understanding towards yourself, even when you make mistakes. It means giving yourself grace and compassion, instead of judgment and criticism.

3. Treat yourself with kindness: We wouldn't dream of treating our loved ones with anything less than kindness, so why do we treat ourselves that way? Start treating yourself with the same kindness and respect that you would give to others. This includes speaking kindly to yourself, taking care of your physical and emotional needs, and doing things that make you happy.

4. Accept yourself: We are all perfectly imperfect human beings, and we all have flaws. Learning to accept yourself just as you are, is an important part of self-love. It means accepting your weaknesses and your strengths, your successes, and your failures. It means accepting all aspects of yourself, without judgment or criticism.

5. Nourish yourself: Just as we need food to nourish our bodies, we also need love and attention to nourish our souls. Start giving yourself the love and care that you deserve. This includes taking time for yourself, doing things that make you happy, and surrounding yourself with positive people.

6. Be mindful of your thoughts and emotions: When you catch yourself being negative, take a step back and reframe your thoughts in a more positive light. For example, instead of thinking "I'm such a failure," try telling yourself "I'm doing the best that I can."

7. Give yourself compliments: We are often quick to point out our flaws, but we should also take the time to acknowledge our strengths and accomplishments. Write down 3 things that you love about yourself each day and refer back to them when you need a confidence boost.

8. Let go of the negative things people have said about you in the past: We all have haters, but it's important to not let their words define you. Instead, focus on the positive things people have said about you and the accomplishments that you have made in your life. These are the things that matter!

9. Most importantly, be patient with yourself: Healing takes time, and there is no timeline for self-love. Give yourself the time and space you need to heal at your own pace and trust that you are exactly where you are supposed to be.

10. Practice gratitude daily: Shift your focus to the things in your life that you are thankful for, such as your health, your family, your friends, etc.

Learning to love yourself unconditionally is a journey, but it is so worth taking. When you love yourself, you open the possibility of also being loved by others. You also create a foundation of strength and resilience that will help you through tough times. So, start today, and begin the journey of self-love.

Healing from trauma

One of the most important benefits of unconditional self-love is that it can help us heal from trauma. Trauma can be incredibly damaging, both mentally and physically. It can leave us feeling overwhelmed and stressed, and it can be difficult to overcome on our own. That's where self-love comes in.

When we can love ourselves unconditionally, we provide ourselves with a safe and supportive space to heal. We allow ourselves to feel our feelings, both good and bad, without judgment. We give ourselves the time and space we need to heal, and we allow ourselves to move on from the trauma. This is an incredible healing process that can help us restore our mental and physical health.

If you are struggling with trauma, please know that you are not alone. And remember that self-love is always available as a source of healing and support. With time and patience, you can begin to heal your trauma and reclaim your life.

The benefits of unconditional self-love
Self-love has a plethora of benefits, including but not limited to:

- **Healing from trauma:** to heal from trauma, it is necessary to love oneself unconditionally. This allows Black Women to connect with their authentic selves and experience true happiness and joy.
- **Contentment and happiness:** Unconditional self-love leads to contentment and happiness because it allows us to see ourselves in a more positive light.
- **Improved relationships:** When we can love ourselves unconditionally, we are also better able to give and receive love from others. This creates a foundation of love and support that is crucial for Black Women.

- **Self-empowerment:** One of the most powerful benefits of self-love is that it allows us to tap into our own inner power and potential. This is an incredibly transformative experience that can help us achieve our goals and dreams.
- **Connecting with our authentic selves:** One of the benefits of self-love is that it allows us to connect with our authentic selves. This is important because it allows us to experience true happiness and joy.
- **Seeing ourselves in a more positive light:** When we love ourselves unconditionally, we begin to see ourselves in a more positive light. This can lead to self-improvement and help us achieve our goals and dreams.
- We can give and receive love from others, giving us a foundation of love and support.

These are just a few of the many benefits that self-love can provide. When we take the time to love and care for ourselves, we open the possibility for incredible growth and transformation. We allow ourselves to experience life in a new and more meaningful way. So, why not give self-love a try? It may be exactly what you need to start living your best life.

FROM TRAUMA TO TRIUMPH

Writing a Love Letter to Yourself

One of the best ways to show yourself some love is by writing a love letter. It can be difficult to know completely if you aren't healed, but it is so worth it! A love letter is a beautiful way to express your thoughts and feelings, without any conditions or expectations. It is a letter of pure self-love, and it can be incredibly healing.

Here are some tips for how to write a love letter to yourself:
1. Start by brainstorming a list of things that you love about yourself. Write down everything that comes to mind, no matter how small or insignificant it may seem.

2. Once you have a list of things that you love about yourself, start writing your letter! Include as many details as possible and be sure to express your love and gratitude.
3. Keep the letter somewhere safe and refer back to it whenever you need a reminder of how amazing you are.

If you find that you can't write a love letter to yourself just yet, that's okay. If you don't feel like you love the version of yourself that you see in the mirror, that's ok too. Start by looking at yourself in the mirror and saying something nice about yourself, even if you don't mean it yet. Every time you pass a mirror, look yourself in the eyes and say something nice (I know that can be hard when you don't like what you see in the mirror). Then allow yourself to feel the love that you are building for yourself; full self-love will come. Focus on the things that you appreciate about yourself, and let those positive feelings fill your heart. Remember, self-love is a journey, and there is no rush. Take your time and be gentle with yourself.

If you can't write that love letter and you can't even say anything nice about yourself, then start by simply repeating loving affirmations to yourself until you can. Affirmations are positive statements that we can say to ourselves to change our mindset and beliefs. When we repeat affirmations frequently, they can help us to believe in ourselves and our ability to achieve our goal of unconditional self-love.

Here are some examples of self-love affirmations:
- I am worthy of love and respect.
- I am allowed to make mistakes.
- I am capable of achieving my goals.
- I am worthy of happiness and joy.
- I love and appreciate myself just as I am.

- I am worthy of love and respect
- I am deserving of happiness
- I am valued and appreciated
- I am not perfect, and that's okay
- I am worthy of forgiveness
- I am allowed to make mistakes
- I am allowed to feel my feelings
- I am doing the best I can
- I am worthy of self-love
- I love and accept myself, unconditionally

Remember, the goal is to repeat these affirmations frequently until they become a part of your belief system. So, find some that resonate with you, and say them out loud every day!

Healing takes time, and you will get there when you are ready.

In the meantime, try to do something nice for yourself every day. This can be something as simple as taking a relaxing bath, going for a walk in nature, or eating your favorite food. Just make sure that you are doing something that makes you feel good! The more love and care you show yourself, the easier it will be to write that love letter.

By LeAnne Dolce

Final Thoughts

Self-love is one of the most important things a Black Woman can give herself, yet it is often one of the hardest things to do. However, it is so worth it! It is an incredibly powerful tool for self-care that can help us heal from trauma, improve our mental and physical health, and live our best life.

When we can love ourselves unconditionally, we open up the possibility for incredible growth and transformation. We provide ourselves with a safe and supportive space to heal. We allow ourselves to feel our feelings, both good and bad, without judgment. We give ourselves the time and space we need to heal, and we allow ourselves to move on from the trauma. We allow ourselves to experience life in a new and more meaningful way.

This incredible healing process helps us restore our mental and physical health. If you are struggling with trauma, please know that you are not alone. And remember that self-love is always available as a source of healing and support. With time and patience, you can begin to heal your trauma and reclaim your life. So, why not give self-love a try? It may be exactly what you need to feel happier and more fulfilled.

Chapter 7
I'm Not Your Superwoman

As Black Women, we are often seen as strong and invincible. We are the backbone of our families and communities and are always expected to be happy and put others first. We don't feel like we are allowed to show weakness because we are the ones that everyone comes to for help. But no one checks on us to see if we need help. We want to break out of this cycle and learn how to love ourselves so that we can heal from the trauma that has been passed down to us. When we are happy, confident, and loving of ourselves, we bring more love and happiness to ourselves because love attracts love.

By LeAnne Dolce

This chapter is about Black women removing the cape they have been wearing for years. They are stepping out of the Superwoman Myth and learning that it's okay to ask for help and be vulnerable. They need to learn that they don't have to be perfect or solve everyone's problems.

When we try to live up to the Superwoman Myth, we often end up overwhelmed, exhausted, and burnt out. We feel guilty when we can't help others and we are constantly trying to do it all. We are afraid of being replaced or not being good enough. This leaves us feeling isolated and unsupported. We need to learn to ask for help and know that it's okay to not be perfect. We are human after all.

How Being Superwoman is Breaking Our Sisters

The Superwoman Myth is hurting Black women because it is causing them to feel overwhelmed, exhausted, and burnt out. They feel guilty when they can't help others and are constantly trying to do it all. They are afraid of being replaced or not being good enough. This leaves them feeling isolated and unsupported. They need to learn to ask for help and know that it's okay to not be perfect. We are human after all.

From Trauma To Triumph

This myth is also preventing Black women from taking care of themselves and their own needs. They often think it's selfish to focus on their well-being, but that couldn't be further from the truth. Self-care is essential for our mental, emotional, and physical health. It helps us stay balanced and connected to our inner strength. Taking time for yourself can provide clarity and help you make better decisions for your life.

Black women need to recognize that they don't have to do it all by themselves; it's okay to ask for help! Start by reaching out to trusted family members or friends if you need support. You can also seek out a therapist or counselor to help you work through your issues and learn how to love yourself.

Make sure that you are taking time for yourself each day, even if it's just 10 minutes. This can be used to meditate, take a walk, listen to music, write in a journal, practice yoga, or do anything else that brings you peace and joy. Engage in activities that make life enjoyable and meaningful.

We know it is hard to break free from the Superwoman Myth, but we can do this together! When we embrace our imperfections and recognize that we need help sometimes, it will bring us closer as sisters. We don't have to carry the weight of the world on our shoulders, and we don't have to do it alone. Let's all remove our capes, come together, and support each other in our journeys. We are powerful beyond measure!

Remember that you deserve love and happiness just as much as anyone else. You have the right to take care of yourself and ask for help when needed. When you make yourself a priority, your life will be more fulfilling and meaningful. So let go of the Superwoman cape and embrace being human - flaws included! Your strength lies within you; unlock it today!

5 tips on how to break free from the superwoman myth
To remove the cape and break free from the Superwoman Myth, we need to learn to love ourselves first. We need to put ourselves first and take care of our own needs. This will allow us to show up in our lives fully present and authentically happy. We also need to join a supportive community like the Sisterhood or the Happiness Mastermind so we can continue to grow, heal, and reconnect to the best version of ourselves.

From Trauma To Triumph

1. Recognize that you don't have to be perfect and it's ok to ask for help. You can't do it all alone so don't be afraid to reach out for support when you need it. Remember that you are not alone on this journey. Others understand what you are going through and can offer support.

2. Connect with your authentic self and learn to love yourself unconditionally. To break free from the Superwoman Myth, we need to connect with our authentic selves. We need to learn to love ourselves unconditionally, regardless of what we do or don't do. When we learn to love ourselves, we can show up in our lives more fully and authentically. We also become more accepting and forgiving of ourselves. This allows us to let go of the guilt and self-judgment that often keep us stuck in the Superwoman Myth.

3. Continue to grow and heal by embracing your vulnerability. One of the best ways to grow and heal is by embracing your vulnerability. When we vulnerably share our stories and feelings, we can connect with others on a deeper level. We also start to see that we are not alone in our struggles. Additionally, when we are open to others, we allow ourselves to experience compassion and support. This can be incredibly healing and transformative. If you are

ready to embrace your vulnerability and continue growing and healing, I invite you to join my upcoming course, "The Art of Vulnerability." In this course, you will learn how to vulnerably share your stories and feelings, connect with others on a deeper level, and experience compassion and support.

4. Make sure to connect with a supportive community like The Sister Circle, either in-person or online, where you can share your experiences and get support. Our community, The Sister Circle is a supportive community for women that offers monthly calls, a private Facebook group, online training, expert calls, and a wealth of other resources. The Sister Circle is a place where women can come together share their stories, support one another, and learn from one another in a judge-free environment. Additionally, being a part of a supportive community will help you to stay accountable to your goals and continue growing and healing.

5. Be kind to yourself, permit yourself to make mistakes, and celebrate your accomplishments. Start taking care of yourself first and make your happiness a priority. Putting ourselves first is a resolution that we can make to break free from the superwoman myth. When we take care of our own

needs, we are better able to show up for others. We become more present and available for those that we love. Additionally, when we take care of ourselves, we are better equipped to handle stress and adversity. We become stronger and more resilient individuals. So, let's commit to putting ourselves first in 2019 and break free from the superwoman myth!

The benefits of breaking free from the Superwoman Myth

When we break free from the Superwoman Myth, we can show up in our lives more authentically. We no longer have to pretend to be someone we're not. We can be ourselves and let our light shine. We also have more time and energy to devote to our own happiness and well-being. We no longer feel overwhelmed and exhausted, and we start to experience more joy and peace in our lives. This is a crucial step on the road to self-love and empowerment. When we learn to love ourselves unconditionally, we can manifest our dreams and goals with ease. We become unstoppable women who know their worth and power.

When we learn to love ourselves unconditionally, we can manifest our dreams and goals with ease. We become unstoppable women who know their worth and power. For this change to happen, first we need to recognize that it's okay not to be perfect or solve everyone's problem single-handedly--that's what makes us human! Join a supportive community like the Sisterhood or Happiness Mastermind so you can continue growing, healing, & reconnecting with your best self!

Our key takeaways include:
1. It's okay to not be perfect, you're human!
2. Join a supportive community so you can continue growing, healing, & reconnecting with your best self.
3. Recognize that you are worthy and deserving of love & happiness.
4. Take care of yourself first to show up authentically in your life.
5. Embrace your vulnerability as it is essential to continued growth.

Conclusion

We know that trying to break free from the Superwoman Myth is hard, but it is possible with love, support, and self-care. We don't have to carry the weight of the world on our shoulders, and we don't have to do it alone. Let us all remove our capes, come together, and support each other in our journeys. When you make yourself a priority, your life will be more fulfilling and meaningful. Trust that you are powerful beyond measure! Make sure to take time for yourself each day and reach out when needed; there is no shame in needing assistance. So let go of the Superwoman cape and embrace being human - flaws and all! Unlock your inner strength today!

You've got this, sis! Keep shining and believing in yourself. We believe in you too! The journey ahead may not be easy but remember that you are strong enough to handle whatever comes your way. You can do this! Believe in yourself – you are amazing! Unlock the power of your feminine energy today – you are powerful beyond measure so now learn to be vulnerable because there is strength in that as well! Now let's go forth and make ourselves a priority for a more fulfilling life ahead.

Keep shining, sis!

By LeAnne Dolce

Chapter 8

Breaking Free from Narcissistic and Toxic Relationships

If you're stuck in a cycle of narcissistic or toxic relationships, this chapter will show you how to break free. You'll learn about the manipulation and mind games that narcissists use to control their victims, and how to protect yourself from these tactics. You'll also find out how to deal with the trauma that often results from these relationships.

It's not easy to break free from a narcissistic or toxic relationship, but it is possible, you may need to take some time for self-care and healing before you're ready to face the challenges of leaving. But eventually, you will need to take action if you want to reclaim your life.

There are many things to consider when breaking free from a narcissistic or toxic relationship. You'll need to prepare yourself emotionally and mentally, as well as physically and financially. You'll also need to have a solid support system in place.

What are narcissistic and toxic relationships?

A narcissistic relationship is one in which one person is completely focused on themselves and their own needs, while the other person is put in a position of always catering to those needs. A toxic relationship is one in which there is a lot of emotional and psychological abuse.

Narcissistic relationships are characterized by a pattern of manipulation and control. Narcissists often use emotional abuse to keep their partners under their thumb. Toxic relationships are generally unhealthy and abusive, often involving one person who is dominant and aggressive, and another who is submissive and compliant.

Narcissistic and toxic relationships can have many negative effects on both partners, some common effects include:

- **Low self-esteem:** Narcissistic and toxic relationships often involve one partner putting the other down constantly. This can lead to the victim having low self-esteem and feeling unworthy of love.

- **Anxiety and depression:** The emotional abuse that often occurs in narcissistic and toxic relationships can cause anxiety and depression.
- **Trauma:** The trauma from being in an abusive relationship can last long after the relationship has ended. It's important to seek help from a therapist or counselor if you're dealing with the aftermath of a toxic relationship.

Signs of a narcissistic or toxic relationship

There are some common signs that you may be in a narcissistic or toxic relationship. If you find yourself always catering to your partner's needs and never being able to put yourself first, that's a red flag. If you're constantly being criticized and put down, or if you're living in fear of your partner's anger, those are also signs that you may be in an unhealthy relationship.

If your partner shows little interest in the emotional world of others and they appear unaware of the impact they have on others, that lack of empathy is a strong indication that you are in a narcissistic or toxic relationship.

If your partner is constantly manipulating and controlling you, then you are likely in a narcissistic or toxic relationship.

Living in a narcissistic or toxic relationship can have several negative consequences for your health and well-being. These types of relationships are often emotionally and psychologically abusive. You may find yourself feeling isolated, alone, and worthless, suffering from anxiety, depression, and low self-esteem. You may also have difficulty trusting other people, and you may find it hard to maintain healthy relationships.

Narcissistic and toxic relationships can also be physically abusive. If you're living in fear of your partner's violence, that's a sign that you're in an unhealthy and dangerous situation.

Protecting Yourself from Narcissistic Manipulation tactics

Narcissists use a variety of manipulation tactics to control their victims. Some of these tactics include:

- **Playing the victim:** Narcissists often play the victim's role to control their partner. They make their partner feel guilty and responsible for all the problems in the relationship. The narcissist will often act like they are the one who is being hurt and wronged, even when they are the one causing harm. This tactic can be very effective in manipulating their partner into staying in the relationship.
- **Gas lighting:** Gas lighting is a technique in which the abuser manipulates the victim into doubting their own memories, perceptions, and sanity. The abuser will often deny doing or saying something that the victim clearly remembers, or they will make subtle changes to conversations so that the victim begins to question their own memory. The goal of gas lighting is to make the victim doubt their own instincts and intuition, ultimately making them more dependent on the abuser. The narcissist wants to be in control of the relationship, and they know that gas lighting is an effective way to achieve that goal. If the victim starts to question their own sanity, they are less likely to leave the relationship or stand up to the abuser.

- **Projecting:** One of the ways that narcissists control their partners is by projecting their own feelings and behavior onto their partner. For example, if the narcissist is feeling angry or resentful, they will accuse their partner of being angry or resentful. If the narcissist is feeling insecure, they will accuse their partner of being insecure. The narcissist will often use projection to deflect blame from themselves and put it on their partner. Projection can also be a way for the narcissist to fuel the drama in the relationship. By accusing their partner of doing or feeling things that they are actually doing or feeling, the narcissist can create conflict and chaos. This allows them to stay in the spotlight and maintain control over their partner.
- **Using guilt and shame:** They may make their partner feel like they're not good enough or that they don't deserve love. Narcissists will often use these tactics to get their partners to do what they want. They may also use them to maintain control over their partner. By making their partner feel guilty or ashamed, the narcissist can keep them in line and stop them from standing up to them.

- **Withholding:** They may give their partner sporadic bursts of love and affection, but then they will quickly withdraw it again. This can leave their partner feeling confused and uncertain. The narcissist does this to maintain control over their partner and keep them in a state of dependence. By withholding love and affection, narcissists can make their partners feel like they are not good enough or that they don't deserve love. They may also use this tactic to punish their partner for challenging them or standing up to them.
- **Manipulative threats:** Narcissists often use manipulative threats to control their partners. Threats can be a very effective way to get what the narcissist wants, and they will often use them to keep their partner in line. The narcissist may threaten to leave the relationship if they don't get what they want. This can be a very effective way to control their partner, as the partner may be afraid of being left alone or having to deal with the pain of a breakup. The narcissist may also threaten to take away their children or commit suicide if their partner doesn't cooperate with them. They may use fear as a way to control their partner. They may intimidate or threaten

their partner with physical violence, or they may make them feel like they are not safe. Narcissists want their partners to be afraid of them, and they will use any means necessary to achieve this goal. Manipulative threats are an effective way for narcissists to control their partners and get what they want. By using threats, narcissists can maintain power and control in the relationship and keep their partner under their thumb.

If you're in a relationship with a narcissist or toxic person, it's important to be aware of these manipulation tactics. You can protect yourself by setting boundaries and not allowing yourself to be controlled. You should also seek out support from friends or family members who can help you through this difficult time.

1. **Be aware of their tactics:** It's important to be aware of the tactics that the narcissist or toxic person uses to protect yourself. This way, you can spot them when they're being used and react accordingly.
2. **Make a plan to leave:** Before you do anything, make a plan. Determine what steps you need to take to safely end the relationship and how long it will take

you to complete them. You need to get your finances in order and find a safe place to stay. If necessary, get in touch with a local domestic violence hotline for additional resources and support. This will help minimize the risk of retaliation.

3. **Document everything:** Document every interaction with them that has been harmful or abusive. This will help provide evidence for later should you need it for legal purposes or to get a restraining order.
4. **Work on rebuilding your self-esteem:** Spend time with people who love and support you, do things that make you happy, and remind yourself that you are worthy of love and respect.
5. **Set boundaries:** You need to set boundaries with the narcissist or toxic person to protect yourself. This means saying no when you don't want to do something, setting limits on how many contacts you have with them, and standing up for yourself.
6. **Get support:** Seek out support from supportive friends or family members or consider seeing a therapist who can help you process the emotional abuse you've experienced.
7. **Focus on healing:** The most important thing is to focus on healing from the abuse. This takes time, but

it's important to be patient with yourself and give yourself the space to heal.

The main challenge of breaking free from a narcissistic or toxic relationship is the emotional and psychological abuse that you may have experienced. This can leave you feeling scared, alone, and unlovable. You may also have financial dependencies that make it difficult to leave.

But it's important to remember that you are not alone. Some people care about you and want to help you through this difficult time. And there are resources available to help you get back on your feet financially.

Breaking free from a narcissistic or toxic relationship is not easy, but it is possible. With the right support system in place, you can start to heal the damage that's been done and rebuild your life on your own terms.

Conclusion

Leaving a narcissistic or toxic relationship can be difficult, but it is worth it. With the right support system in place, you can start to heal the damage that's been done and rebuild your life on your own terms. The first step is reaching out for help; Talk to a friend or family member for support, talk to a therapist, and make a plan to leave. Reach out to a local domestic violence hotline for additional resources and support. Remember, you are not alone. Some people care about you and want to help you through this difficult time. There are resources available to help you get back on your feet financially and emotionally. With the right support, you can make it through this difficult time and come out stronger on the other side.

Chapter 9

Your Ultimate Self-Care Toolkit

The final stop on our journey to waking up happy every day is creating your ultimate Self-Care Toolkit. Self-care is essential for everyone, especially those who are trying to improve their lives. When you take care of yourself, you allow yourself to focus on your goals and dreams. You also become more resilient in the face of stress and setbacks.

But self-care can be difficult to do on your own. That's why it's important to build your self-care toolkit. A self-care toolkit is a collection of strategies, affirmations, items/ products, activities, and other resources that can be used to promote and maintain physical, mental, and emotional well-being. The contents of a self-care toolkit will vary from person to person but may include things like journaling supplies, relaxation techniques, healthy coping mechanisms, and more. This chapter will help you identify the right things to place in your ultimate self-care toolkit.

How to fill your self-care toolkit?

That's the million-dollar question. There is no one-size-fits-all answer to this question, as the contents of your self-care toolkit will be unique to you and your individual needs. However, some general tips can be helpful when putting together your self-care toolkit:

1. Start with the basics: Identify the basics items that you need to feel physically and emotionally safe, comfortable, and grounded in difficult times. These may include things like your favorite books, weighted blankets, journaling supplies, food, water, shelter, and mental health apps.

2. Identify your needs: Once you have the basics covered, take some time to identify your specific needs. What do you need to feel happy, healthy, and well-balanced? This may include things like regular exercise, time for hobbies and relaxation, and a supportive social network.

3. Make a plan: Once you know what you need, make a plan for how you will get it. This may involve setting aside time each day for self-care, stocking your home with healthy snacks and comfortable clothing, or making sure to schedule regular check-ups with your doctor.

4. Reach out for support: Don't forget to include people who can help support your self-care journey in your toolkit. Whether it's a therapist, close friend, family member, or someone else who can lend an ear and offer advice when needed. Friends can offer emotional support and help you stay accountable for your goals. A therapist can help you identify healthy coping mechanisms and develop a plan for managing your symptoms.

5. Focus on prevention: As motivational speakers like Lisa Nichols and Iyanla Vanzant have said many times - don't wait until the storm is upon you to build your protection. Consider the things that help prevent overwhelming stress, anxiety, and depression – such as adequate sleep, exercise, time outdoors in nature, healthy eating habits, and positive affirmations.

6. Be flexible: Remember that your needs may change over time, so be prepared to adjust your self-care toolkit accordingly. If something isn't working for you anymore, don't be afraid to try something new.

7. Be patient with yourself: Making changes to your lifestyle can be difficult, so be patient with yourself as you work on filling your self-care toolkit. Allow yourself time to adjust to new routines and don't be too hard on yourself if you make a mistake. Just get back up and try again!

5. Keep it practical: Your self-care toolkit should be easy to access and use when you need it. That means stocking items and activities that are simple and practical, such as a few favorite self-care books, relaxation techniques, your preferred type of exercise equipment or clothing, meditation music, etc.

What Can I Put in My Self-Care Toolkit?
Remember: Self-care is personal and unique to every individual, so don't forget to make your self-care toolkit

your own. Fill it with items and activities that make you feel balanced, calm, and energized. With the right tools in hand, you'll be on your way to creating a happier life for yourself—one that starts with self-love and care every day.

When thinking of the various items that you can put into your self-care toolkit, it's often helpful to think in terms of the 8 Dimensions of Self-Care to help you pick a variety of items to create your ultimate self-care toolkit.

This can include:
- A journal or self-care workbook available at DolceandLay.com
- Comfortable clothes
- Healthy snacks
- Relaxation techniques (e.g., yoga, meditation, deep breathing exercises)
- Favorite books or movies
- Tilted Crown Affirmation Cards available at DolceandLay.com
- Essential oils
- Candles
- Your favorite wine or drink
- A weighted blanket

- Earplugs or noise-canceling headphones
- Stress balls/fidget toys
- Mental health apps
- Art supplies (e.g., coloring books, sketch pads)
- Music player with calming songs
- Hot tea or other soothing drinks
- List of people you can call for support in difficult times
- List of activities you enjoy (e.g., walks, bike rides, reading)
- Items that remind you of happy memories or experiences
- Vouchers to your favorite café/restaurant/store
- Photos of loved ones or special places
- A copy of your insurance information
- A copy of your personal health records (e.g., prescription details, medical history, etc.)
- Scented candles or incense sticks
- Aromatherapy oils and diffusers
- Massage tools (e.g., foam rollers, back massagers)
- Bath salts or essential oils for a relaxing bath
- Fluffy blankets or pillows for comfort and warmth

I have my Self-Care Toolkit list, now what?

Now that you have your Self-Care Toolkit list, how do you use it? Here are some tips to get started:

1. Use your toolkit to relax: After a long day at work, spend some time relaxing with your self-care tools. Take a hot bath, read your favorite book, or listen to calming music.

2. Use your toolkit to reduce stress: When you're feeling overwhelmed or stressed, use your self-care tools to help you relax and de-stress. Take some deep breaths, go for a walk or journal about your feelings.

3. Use your toolkit to cope with anxiety: If you're struggling with anxiety, use your self-care tools to help you cope. Practice relaxation techniques, exercise, or talk to a therapist.

4. Use your toolkit to boost your mood: When you're feeling down, use your self-care tools to help you boost your mood. Do something you enjoy, reach out to a friend, or treat yourself to something special.

5. Use your toolkit to manage your symptoms: If you're dealing with a mental health issue, use your self-care tools to help you manage your symptoms. Seek professional help, talk to a support group, or follow a treatment plan.

6. Use your toolkit to prevent relapses: If you're in recovery from a mental illness, use your self-care tools to help prevent relapses. Attend therapy sessions, take medication as prescribed, and develop a support system.

Schedule out your Self-Care

Here is a list of daily, weekly, and monthly ways you can plan your self-care events or activities. The goal is to have a designated time and place to practice self-care.

Daily:

- Wake up 10 minutes earlier to meditate, stretch, or journal
- Spend 15 minutes reading your favorite book before bed
- Take a quick walk around the block during lunch break
- Take a hot bath
- Read your favorite book
- Write in your journal

- Listen to calming music

Weekly:

- - Go for a 30-minute run or jog
- Set aside an hour to work on a hobby or creative project
- Attend a yoga class with friends once a week
- Get a massage or take a yoga class
- Have dinner with friends or family members
- Volunteer at a local charity or organization

Monthly:

- Participate in a monthly therapy session
- Take a long weekend trip with your family and friends
- Schedule a massage, mani/Pedi, or other spa treatments
- Join a club and go for a walk outdoors
- Stay up late watching your favorite show/movie marathon
- 'Treat yourself' to something special that you enjoy (i.e. buy a new book, get a manicure/pedicure, etc.)
- Visit a mental health professional (therapist, counselor, doctor)

By LeAnne Dolce

A reminder of why self-care is important and the benefits you will experience by practicing it.

Self-care is important because it allows you to take time for yourself and focus on your well-being. When you practice self-care, you will experience the following benefits:

- Improved mental health and well-being
- Reduced stress and anxiety
- Better sleep quality
- Increased productivity
- Stronger relationships with family and friends

Thank you for reading! We hope this chapter has inspired you to make self-care a priority in your life. It's not always easy, but it is worth it. Remember to use your self-care tools regularly, be patient with yourself as you make changes to your lifestyle and seek professional help if necessary. With time and effort, you can create a life you love and is filled with self-care.

How to Join the Wake Up Happy, Sis Network!

If you are looking for a network of like-minded women who are ready to join you on your journey to waking up happy every day, then you need to join the Wake Up Happy, Sis network. Simply head on over to wakeuphappysis.com and sign up! Once you're registered, you'll have access to a wealth of resources including articles, videos, and e-books on self-care. You can also join our online community of sisters who are dedicated to living a happy and healthy life. We hope to see you soon!

Final thoughts on filling your self-care toolkit

Self-care is an important part of maintaining good mental health. The more you practice self-care and make it a priority in your life, the better off you will be. So, take some time to fill up your Self-Care Toolkit today and schedule out when you'll put into practice all that you have learned. Remember, you deserve to take care of yourself!

But the journey doesn't end here; it's just the beginning. Don't forget to look for additional resources that can help support your self-care journeys such as online blogs, apps, and books – many of which are available at no cost or low cost. You don't have to do this alone! With your new Self-Care Toolkit in hand, you can find the strength to keep going and continue growing. Good luck!

The contents of your Self-Care Toolkit may change over time, but it's important to remember that taking care of yourself is an ongoing journey by filling your toolkit with the right items and activities, you'll be more prepared to take on life's challenges and come out stronger on the other side, also be sure to check in with yourself regularly and make adjustments as needed. You are worth it!

Happy self-care!

Resources for finding more information on self-care

1. The Sister Circle Community is a group of Black women who support and encourage one another in their healing and self-care journeys.

2. The Soul Renewal Experience website provides information on healing and self-care retreats specifically for Black women.

3. The Wake Up Happy Facebook Group is an online support group for Black women who are committed to their healing and self-care journey.

4. The Self-Care Haven is an online resource that provides information and support for Black women on their journey to self-care.

5. Black Women's Health & Wellness is a website that provides information on health and wellness specifically for Black women.

6. The National Black Women's Health Imperative is a national organization that works to improve the health and wellness of Black women.

7. Wellness For All is a website that provides information on health and wellness for people of all backgrounds.

8. The Centers for Disease Control and Prevention is a government agency that provides information on health and wellness for all people.

9. The National Institutes of Health is a government agency that provides information on health and wellness for all people.

10. The World Health Organization is a global organization that provides information on health and wellness for all people.

These are just a few of the many resources available to help Black women on their journey to self-care. With the right support and information, any woman can make self-care a priority in her life.

Conclusion

The book From Trauma to Triumph: The Black Woman's Journey to Waking Up Happy Every Day covers the importance of self-care for black women, the power of feminine energy, healing from past trauma, and learning to love oneself unconditionally. It also provides tips for setting healthy boundaries and breaking free from narcissistic and toxic relationships. We learned that self-care is essential for black women as they face unique challenges, that the power of feminine energy can help heal trauma, and that self-love is the key to happiness.

We've learned that self-care is important for black women and is essential for healing from past trauma. It is also important for setting and maintaining healthy boundaries and breaking free from narcissistic and toxic relationships.

We've also learned about the Superwoman Myth, and how to break free from it.

In Chapter 1, we set the foundation for self-care. We learned that Self-care is the practice of taking care of oneself, both physically and emotionally. It is an important part of maintaining our overall health and well-being, and it helps us to take care of our thoughts and feelings. We also learned that there is no one size fits all approach to self-care – it must be customized to fit the unique needs of the individual. We wrapped the chapter learning how the 8 Dimensions of Self-care allow us to make our self-care a priority.

In Chapter 2, we learned that self-care is vital for black women. Black Women often take on the roles of mother, father, breadwinner, and caretaker for our families, as well as often being the emotional support for friends and loved ones. They deserve to be happy, healed, and filled with self-love without it being for the benefit of others.

In Chapter 3, we learned that feminine energy is creative, intuitive, and expressive. It is the force that motivates us to connect with others and to create meaningful lives. To harness the power of your feminine energy, you must first clear away the blocks that are preventing you from accessing this powerful force within yourself. Feminine energy is often misunderstood because it is so different from masculine energy, which dominates our world. Masculine energy is focused on action and achieving goals while feminine energy is about flow and receptivity.

In Chapter 4, we discussed how Black women often struggle with past trauma, which can lead to several negative consequences in their lives. We learned that it is essential that Black women learn to heal themselves to move forward in life with happiness and peace. We learned what trauma is and how we can help heal ourselves. We learned the connection between trauma, setting healthy boundaries, and incorporating self-care as a part of the healing journey.

Chapter 5 is all about learning to love yourself unconditionally. We discussed how self-love has a plethora of benefits, including but not limited to healing from trauma, contentment, and happiness, improved relationships, self-empowerment, and connecting with our authentic selves. We learned the power of writing a love letter to yourself or when you can't use affirmations to build up your self-love level.

This is important because often we are our own worst critics and don't give ourselves the love that we deserve.

In Chapter 6, we discuss that healthy boundaries are the limits we set to protect ourselves emotionally and mentally. We provided examples of healthy boundaries and discussed how Black women often have difficulty setting boundaries because they are taught to be caretakers and selfless. We learned the 7 types of boundaries, examples of healthy boundaries, and the benefits of having healthy boundaries in the healing process.

In Chapter 7, we meet the Black Woman as Superwoman. They are seen as strong and invincible, but this comes at a cost because they are not allowed to be vulnerable or need help. They are expected to always be happy and put others first, which can lead to burnout, frustration, and anger. We teach Black Women how to embrace their vulnerability as an essential path on their growth journey.

In Chapter 8, we tackle being stuck in a cycle of narcissistic or toxic relationships. We learned about the manipulation and mind games that narcissists use to control their victims, and how to protect yourself from these tactics. We finished by providing steps to build up your self-esteem, and the importance of setting boundaries for narcissistic and toxic people in our lives.

In Chapter 9, we finish the book by helping you fill out your self-care toolkit. As self-care can be difficult to do on your own, we provided the blueprint for creating your self-care toolkit — a collection of strategies and activities that help you take care of yourself. We encourage you to use your self-care tools regularly and be creative with what you put in them. We also talk about the importance of seeking professional help if you are struggling to cope with a mental and emotional health issue. Get support from friends and family as you work on filling your self-care toolkit. Be patient with yourself as you make changes to improve your life.

Self-care is essential for everyone, especially those who are trying to improve their lives. To make self-care a part of your life, start by making small changes in your daily routine to make it a priority. Use your self-care tools regularly and be creative with them. Seek professional help if you are struggling to cope with a mental health issue. Get support from friends and family as you work on filling your self-care toolkit. Be patient with yourself as you make changes to improve your life.

If you are looking for a supportive community to continue your self-care journey, we recommend the Sister Circle community. Join the Sister Circle community to connect with other Black women who are dealing with similar issues. This community is a safe space where you can share your stories, find support, and learn from others. As a member of the Sister Circle, you'll have access to resources, advice, and guidance from experts. You'll also be able to join discussions and participate in events. Join the Sister Circle today to start your journey to healing and happiness.

These key takeaways from the book will help you move forward in your self-care journey.

1. Self-care is important for black women and is essential for healing from past trauma.

Self-care is important for black women and is essential for healing from past trauma. This means that it is crucial for black women to make time for themselves and to practice self-care regularly. This will help them to heal any past trauma they may have experienced and will also allow them to set healthy boundaries and break free from narcissistic and toxic relationships.

2. Feminine energy can be harnessed to help with self-healing.

The second takeaway from the book is that feminine energy can be harnessed to help with self-healing. This means that by tapping into the power of the feminine, black women can begin to heal any trauma they have experienced. The feminine energy is associated with compassion, nurturing, and healing, so by accessing this energy, black women can begin to move through their trauma and start to feel better.

3. Unconditional self-love is key to happiness.

The third and final takeaway from the book is that unconditional self-love is key to happiness. This means that to be truly happy, black women need to learn to love themselves unconditionally. This means accepting themselves for who they are, flaws and all. Once black women can do this, they will begin to feel happier and more content with their lives.

3. Loving yourself unconditionally is key to happiness

The third and final takeaway from the book is that unconditional self-love is key to happiness. This means that to be truly happy, black women need to learn to love themselves unconditionally. This means accepting themselves for who they are, flaws and all. Once black women can do this, they will begin to feel happier and more content with their lives.

4. Setting healthy boundaries is necessary for a healthy life

Black women need to set healthy boundaries to have a healthy life. This means that they need to learn how to say no, and how to protect themselves from harm. They also need to learn how to take care of themselves, and how to put their needs first. By doing this, black women will be better able to protect themselves from the harmful things that may happen in their lives.

Thank you for reading! I hope you found the information in this book helpful and informative. I hope that you are on the road to being happy, healed, and whole! I would love to hear your thoughts on the book, so please feel free to share your comments and leave a review.

By LeAnne Dolce

Wake Up Happy, Sis! Network

Wake Up Happy, Sis! is a network specifically designed for dynamic and vibrant high performing and high achieving Black Women. We offer safe and supportive spaces where Black Women can come together to share their stories, connect with others, and find inspiration to live their best lives. WUHS places a high emphasis on self-care and healing from past traumas, which are often overlooked or ignored in high achieving environments.

At the core of the Wake Up Happy, Sis! Network is a commitment to helping Black Women find their voice and cultivate their inner strength to put themselves first in their lives, while addressing the unique challenges they may face in their personal and professional lives. Through personal stories, expert advice, online training, and interviews with inspiring Black Women, the network offers a wealth of resources to help high achieving Black Women overcome obstacles, heal past traumas, and wake up happy every day so they can achieve their goals and live the lives of their dreams.

Self-care is a central theme in the Wake Up Happy, Sis! Network, we recognize the importance of taking care of yourself to thrive in a high-performance environment where you are being pulled in all directions at once and rarely have time to stop and focus on yourself. Practical tips and strategies based on the 8 dimensions of self-care are provided in abundance. Additionally, the network offers support and guidance for healing from past traumas, which are often overlooked in high achieving environments but can have a significant impact on your overall well-being.

The Wake Up Happy, Sis! Network also addresses a variety of topics that timely and relevant to high performing Black Women, such as imposter syndrome, navigating corporate environments, setting boundaries, and building supportive networks. With a team of contributors who are all dedicated to empowering Black Women and promoting positive change, the Wake Up Happy, Sis! Network is a source of inspiration and motivation for Black Women who are striving to reach their full potential.

In addition to its online content, the network also hosts a range of events specifically tailored for high performing Black Women, including workshops, meetups, VIP days, and wellness retreats. These events provide opportunities for Black Women to connect with others in person, build relationships, and learn new skills in a supportive environment.

The Wake Up Happy, Sis! Network is more than a community. We are a platform that provides a supportive system and community for high performing and high achieving Black Women with a range of valuable resources to help you achieve your goals and improve your lives. Here are just a few examples of the resources available:

1. **Wake Up Happy, Sis! Website:** The website is your entry to the Wake Up Happy, Sis! Network. Access www.WakeUpHappySis.com to learn more about each of the resources listed below and read our blog posts to keep you engaged with wellness tips and techniques from our contributors.

2. **Wake Up Happy, Sis! FREE Facebook Group:** The free Facebook group provides a community of supportive Black Women who share their stories, offer advice, and connect with one another. Members can

participate in discussions, ask for support, and find inspiration to pursue their dreams.

3. **The Sister Circle Paid Community:** The Sister Circle is a paid membership community that offers access to a range of exclusive content, including workshops, live streams, expert advice, digital wellness resources and private coaching sessions. Members of The Sister Circle also have access to a private Facebook group and networking opportunities.

4. **The Wake Up Happy Sis Show:** The Wake Up Happy Sis Show is a weekly radio show and podcast that streams on all podcasting platforms, YouTube, Facebook, and LinkedIn every Monday at 10am EST. The show features interviews with inspiring Black Women, expert advice, and practical tips for achieving balance and harmony in your personal and professional life.

5. **The Soul Renewal Experience Retreats:** The Soul Renewal Experience Retreats are immersive retreats that offer Black Women the opportunity to connect with themselves and other Black Women in a supportive and

nurturing environment. These retreats provide a space for healing, personal growth, and self-discovery.

6. **Soul Renewal VIP Days:** Soul Renewal VIP Days are one-day events that offer high-level coaching, training, and support for Black Women who are looking to take their lives and careers to the next level. These events provide one-on-one coaching sessions and personalized support to help Black Women achieve their goals.

7. **Dolce & Lay Personal Pampering skincare products and accessories:** The Dolce & Lay Personal Pampering product line offers high-quality skincare products and accessories to help Black Women take care of themselves and feel their best. The product line includes items such as face masks, body scrubs, and moisturizers.

8. **InspHERation apparel and personal discovery items:** This product line offers a range of apparel and personal discovery items that are designed to inspire and motivate Black Women to achieve their goals. The product line includes items such as t-shirts, journals, and inspirational wall art.

Overall, the Wake Up Happy, Sis! Network provides Black Women with a wealth of resources to help them become and stay HAPPY, HEALED, AND WHOLE. Whether it's through the free Facebook group, paid membership group, podcasts, retreats, or product lines, the network offers a supportive and empowering community where Black Women can find the motivation, guidance, and resources they need to put themselves first, heal, and thrive, not just exist.

By LeAnne Dolce

About LeAnne Dolce

LeAnne Dolce is a long-time student of the wellness arts, a self-care accountability coach, and a certified product formulator.

In her early 30s, LeAnne woke up and found herself in a state of depression. She was morbidly obese, overwhelmed, and feeling majorly defeated. She knew from that day that she had to literally change or die. For many of us, we are at that same crossroads where we must change or die trying, but you feel like if you do, so many other people are going to be hurt if you change, what about your spouse, your kids, and your business? You feel like the whole world depends on you! What LeAnne had to learn was how to prioritize herself first. Today, she helps other Black Women prioritize their self-care and wellness for themselves, not to be a better mother, wife, or boss. But to be a better person for yourself first. LeAnne created The Wake Up Happy, Sis! Network for Black women to help them reconnect with their feminine energy and heal from past trauma so they can live their best lives without guilt in a supportive environment.

www.ingramcontent.com/pod-product-compliance
Lightning Source LLC
LaVergne TN
LVHW020934090426
835512LV00020B/3349